u.
icomp
 when c
can take c
ote compat.
tain trouble-.
ease the total c

morality, called "rat.
I to almost everyone, bec
he satisfaction of (universa.,
ly everyone has; because it is
oring no person or group over
cause it offers protection
v of the majority. And
provides a method
agreements.

MORALS WITHOUT MYSTERY

MORALS WITHOUT MYSTERY

A Liberating Alternative
to Established Morality
based on Bertrand Russell's Views
applied to Current Problems

by
LEE EISLER

PHILOSOPHICAL LIBRARY
New York

Morals Without Mystery is based on Bertrand Russell's views, chiefly as expressed in his *Human Society in Ethics and Politics*, published (outside the USA) by Allen & Unwin and (in the USA) by Simon & Schuster. Permission has been given to use material from the Russell book.

MORALS WITHOUT MYSTERY is a well-written short presentation of the kind of morality I believe in and advocate.

Bertrand Russell

Table of Contents

Introduction

Introduction

This book presents arguments in favor of a certain system of morality.

Even people who have no particular interest in problems of morality will nevertheless have notions that certain acts are right and others wrong. You may or may not care whether unmarried people have sex relations, but you will not think that rape is permissible. That is because you have a code of morality. And since we all have *some* code of morality, it is well to have one that can withstand scrutiny.

The system of morality presented here is essentially Bertrand Russell's. It is he who found a way out of the wilderness; I merely follow his guideposts. The erudition is his too. When I mention why the ancient Spartans approved of homosexuality, or cite St. Thomas' arguments against divorce and incest, or tell why Uzzah was struck dead, it is Russell's learning that supplies these instances.

In my imagination, I can hear someone saying to Russell: "The world is a mess, full of hungry, miserable people. No one cares about them, or about mankind in general; people care only about themselves, their families, and their friends. Some people will always take advantage of others, the strong will conquer the weak, big nations will impose their will on small nations. In view of all this, I see no prospect of things ever improving in the world, no likelihood of increasing mankind's happiness, because people will behave no better in the future than they have in the past. Have you any comment to make on this rather pessimistic outlook, Lord Russell?"

And I imagine I can hear Russell reply: "Well, I agree that the world is a mess, full of hunger and misery. And I agree that people seem to care only for their own, and in any event, their concern for others rarely extends beyond the borders of their own country. And certainly, if men continue to act in future as they have in the past, they are indeed doomed, not merely to unhappiness, but to extinction by H-bombs.

"There is, however, a way out of the mess that can lead to such an enormous increase in happiness that few people today are able even to imagine it; yet it is entirely within our grasp. To achieve it, men have only to use their intelligence to see where their true interests lie, to act in ways that promote those interests, and to refrain from acting in ways that endanger them. That, I think, is what we ought to try to do."

And Russell, in various books, has shown us how to do it.

But why should anyone want to rewrite Russell since he writes so superbly himself? (He won a Nobel Prize for *literature* in 1950.)

It is true that Russell is the most widely read philosopher of modern times; his books are translated into many languages; his renown is world-wide. Yet it cannot be said that most people know his views on morality or even know that he, thought and wrote a great deal about this subject over a period of 50 years. In fact, the average American is more likely to associate Russell's name with immorality than morality, as a result of the 1940 propaganda campaign that vilified him (chiefly because he had written "Marriage and Morals") and that culminated in the lawsuit that barred Russell from teaching mathematical logic at the College of the City of New York (CCNY), on the grounds that he would corrupt the young.

I have rewritten Russell because I find his ideas on morality enlightening and liberating; because I find that most people don't seem to know about them; and because we would all be better off if they did.

I have taken Russell's ideas on morality, as I understand them, chiefly from his "Human Society in Ethics and Politics" (1955). "Morals without Mystery" (a) does not explore as many byways, and is considerably shorter and, I think, simpler; (b) its tone is different, less like a book on philosophy and more like one on applied navigation; (c) it examines a number of contemporary moral problems, to demonstrate how the system works as well as to arrive at answers to the problems.

I have taken liberties—I have added as well as omitted—

but I like to think that I may be bringing some of Russell's wisdom to people who otherwise might not come across it, and perhaps even tempt them into reading Russell in the original. I know of nothing more rewarding. It is always a delight to see his mind at work, reducing some mystery to its essential elements and then fitting the elements together so that they make sense. Life is a jigsaw puzzle of such engulfing size that few people ever succeed in assembling more than a few of the pieces; Russell fits almost all of them into a coherent whole in a convincing and satisfying way that no one else I know of has been able to do.

Many friends have helped me with this book, in many ways, and I am indebted to all of them: to Alex and Nancy Crosby, to Abe Friedman, to Jeanne and Bill Gorham, to Jean Hollyman, to Helen Papashvily, to Hans Rosenhaupt, and most particularly to Tracy Samuels, for her many suggestions that improved the manuscript and for generously giving so much of her time. I also wish to thank Christopher Farley, of The Bertrand Russell Peace Foundation, Ltd. (London), for his many helpful trans-Atlantic letters. And not least of all, my thanks go to Miz, who had to do so many other things while I was doing this.

Principles

1. Morality and malaise.

"I'm tired of wealthy people who give their children cars, but no moral values, coming to me and saying they don't know what's wrong with their youngsters," said Dr. Benjamin B. Wolman, a professor of psychology and psychoanalyst, in what turned out to be the Quotation of the Day in the New York Times of October 19, 1967.

"What is wrong is that the parents are leading hollow empty lives and not giving their children anything to hold onto," said Dr. Wolman.

Parental permissiveness masks the fact that these parents have no particular moral norms they care to pass along, he said.

"The new generation is rebelling against the nothingness they see breeding in the suburbs . . . against the nihilism they see around them," said the doctor.

The Times story did not report what kind of moral values Dr. Wolman thought parents ought to give their children, to fill the vacuum. That, no doubt, is the core of the problem.

What kind of morality *can* a 20th century man pass along to his children? Is conventional morality acceptable in the light of present-day knowledge?

2. The Bible as a source of morality.

The two bases of conventional morality most widely re-
lied on, or most often cited in defending a particular act as
moral, are the Bible and conscience. Let us look first at the
Bible.

The Bible contains the two best-known and most influential
statements on morality in the Western world—the Ten Commandments and the Sermon on the Mount. We are not at this
point considering the merits of the morality they present but
whether the fact that they came from the Bible is sufficient
reason for accepting them.

The Bible says the world was created in 6 days (Genesis
1:1-31), but geologists now estimate that, for example, it
took millions of years to create a geographical feature such as
the Mississippi Delta. The Bible tells us that God created the
various separate and distinct species of animals on a single
day (Genesis 1:20-23), but the theory of evolution, which
may now be taught even in Tennessee, holds that they all
evolved from a remote common ancestor over millions of
years. The Bible also says, "Thou shalt not suffer a witch to
live," (Exodus 22:18) which, to begin with, requires us to
believe in the existence of witches.

I do not see how, in the light of present-day knowledge,
it is possible to believe in the literal truth of the Bible.

If some or all of the morality presented in the Bible is to
be judged worthy of acceptance, it will have to be on some
basis other than that it comes from the Bible.

3. Conscience as a source of morality.

Conscience is another bulwark of morality. If a man says, "I follow the dictates of my conscience, regardless of consequences," this is generally admired in our society; but not always. When a draftee refuses to fight in Viet Nam because his conscience tells him that this particular war is immoral, many see nothing admirable in it at all, and say it is wrong of him to refuse to bear arms for his country—even though his position is unassailable in the sense that they cannot prove that his conscience does not tell him what he claims it does.

Some people's consciences tell them that the mercy killings of euthanasia are morally right, other people's consciences tell them the opposite, on the ground that it is never right for one human being to put an end to another human being's life. The people who advance this argument do not necessarily advance it against the killings in Viet Nam.

A puritan's conscience will tell its possessor that pleasure is bad, whereas a utilitarian's will say it is good.

As these examples show, conscience, if accepted as a basis of morality, produces moral anarchy. Consciences disagree, and if every man is to follow his own conscience, there is no basis for urging or compelling agreement among people with differing consciences. You could not even ask everyone to heed the best conscience in the community, for there is no way to prove that one man's conscience is superior to another's, except by some standard other than conscience.

We must therefore discard conscience as a basis for a workable morality.

I do not mean that conscience is never relevant to moral issues. I mean that Mr. A will not follow Mr. B's conscience in preference to his own, nor conversely will Mr. B follow Mr. A's; and if they are to be able to get along with each other (and reach agreement on moral issues), the system by which they arrive at their moral decisions will have to be based on something other than conscience.

4. Requirements of an acceptable morality.

Thus far, we have ruled out the Bible as a reliable basis of morality, since it contains statements now known or believed to be untrue; and we have ruled out conscience on the grounds that it is unworkable.

This suggests that a moral code may be acceptable if it is (a) intellectually respectable, and (b) workable.

By "intellectually respectable," I mean it must be compatible with current knowledge, including the findings of science, whatever they may prove to be; it must not be in danger of being upset by some new scientific discovery, any more than scientific method itself is.

To be "workable" it must provide a way of dealing with disagreements. It must also, as we shall see, appeal to the majority of men, and not make impossible demands of them—demands they are not likely to fulfill.

5. Everyone has some code of morality.

Morality provides standards of conduct that govern (or at any rate, influence) our behavior. It also tells how we expect others to behave.

Morality usually consists of a set of rules or principles, by which actions can be judged right or wrong, and therefore acceptable or unacceptable. Every group always has a code of morality governing acceptable behavior.

All of us no doubt consider it wrong to steal and kill. But even outlaws who steal and kill have their morality. If you are a member of a gang of bank robbers, and hold out some of the loot from your fellow gang-members, they will—if they find out about it—be outraged, and will punish you in some suitable way, for not having lived up to their rules of acceptable conduct.

6. Morality and the criminal law.

Our behavior is influenced by the criminal law as well as by the moral code.

We usually don't do what the criminal law forbids because we don't wish to incur the penalty. I don't drive my car faster than the law allows because I don't want to risk losing my driver's license.

But the criminal law does not cover as great an area of human activity as does the moral code. Perhaps in a theocracy, where church and state are identical, the criminal law and the moral code would be identical too; but not in our kind of society.

Ideally, in our society, everything illegal would be immoral. Then the criminal law would be in complete harmony with the moral code. And there is in fact harmony between the criminal code and the moral code with respect to a great many acts, such as stealing, killing, and lying under oath.

Harmony was absent, however, during the Prohibition Era, when many people did not think it immoral to buy liquor from a bootlegger, though it was obviously illegal. There is conflict today between the two codes regarding homosexual acts, which are clearly illegal in most states, but no longer clearly immoral since the taint of immorality was removed, at least for some, at a recent Episcopal conference. Probably the criminal law eventually catches up with the moral code (or at any rate with the prevailing moral feeling), as it did in the case of Prohibition, and as it probably will with homosexuality.

Everything immoral is not illegal. The prevailing morality, for instance, tells you to love your neighbor, but the law does not require it. In fact, your neighbor can be drowning and call to you, sitting on the river bank, for help, which, let us say, you could easily give by throwing him the rope alongside of you, but the law does not require you to lift a

22

finger. When pickets carry signs saying UNFAIR, they are not protesting against some illegal act or condition, but against some alleged transgression of the moral code, at least as they interpret it.

7. Questions for morality to answer.

To return to morality and the service it performs (or ought to):

In most situations in everyday life, the moral issues are clear-cut, and deciding what is moral is no problem. Usually it is clearly wrong to lie, steal or kill.

From time to time, however, situations arise where the moral decision is not easy. We have already mentioned a few of these:

Is the war in Viet Nam moral or immoral?

Is refusing to fight in this war, on grounds of conscience or moral conviction, right or wrong?

Are euthanasia killings morally right or wrong?

Is pleasure morally good or bad?

Was it moral or immoral to buy liquor from a bootlegger during Prohibition?

Is it moral to ignore your neighbor's cry for help?

There are many other questions, too, which it seems highly desirable to find right answers to; yet answers are not obvious or easy to come by, and in any case, do not win general agreement—questions such as these:

Does the end justify the means?
Is selfishness wrong?
Is war immoral?

Was it morally right to drop the A-bomb on Japan?
Is it wrong to cheat on your taxes?
Is it wrong to cheat on exams?

Is cheating on exams wrong, if everyone else is cheating?
Is it wrong to take drugs?
Is human life sacred?

Do men have inalienable rights?
Is man naturally good or bad?
Can human nature change?

Is it morally right to punish criminals?
Is it morally right for Detroit to build high-powered cars?

Nor does this exhaust the kinds of questions that an acceptable morality ought to be able to deal with.

8. More questions for morality to answer.

There are also questions of another sort, related to the whole problem of morality in the modern world, such as these:

> If morality is relative, in the sense that what is considered moral in one place (or in one era or in one group) is not moral in another—devout Christians will work on Saturdays but not on Sundays, devout Jews do just the opposite; Pope Pius IX said that man has no moral obligation to animals, but Hindus worship them —why should we feel bound to obey *any* code of morality?
>
> Should a parent ask his child to accept conventional morality, if he does not believe in it himself?
>
> If you cannot accept conventional morality, does that make you immoral?

An acceptable moral system—one that is workable and intellectually respectable—ought to be able to provide answers to all the questions we have been raising. To be workable, it must, among other things, be able to answer the following:

> How can I tell what's right?
> Why should I do what's right?
> How can the other fellow be made to do what's right?

Can an acceptable system of morality be found, that will meet all these requirements? I suggest that the answer—to be found on the following pages—is yes.

9. Prescribed morality.

One characteristic of traditional morality—most of ours comes from the Bible—is that it tells you what to do (or what *not* to do) but it doesn't tell why.

It gives rules but not reasons:

> Don't commit adultery. Don't work on the Sabbath. Be meek and merciful. Don't desire a woman. Don't divorce your wife (except perhaps for adultery). Don't steal, kill, lie or swear. Don't resist evil. Turn the other cheek. Love your enemies.

The purposes of these rules of behavior—taken from the Ten Commandments and the Sermon on the Mount—are not stated. They are merely prescribed, the way a doctor might prescribe medicine, and as if the doctor had said, "Take the medicine; it's good for you. Don't ask questions; Doctor knows best."

We will call this kind of morality "prescribed morality."

If some or all of prescribed morality is to be acceptable, it will have to be on some basis other than that it has been prescribed—whether by ancient tradition, sacred book, or Divine Command.

10. Rules of morality with purpose unknown.

Prescribed morality usually fails to state its aims, and this leads to serious difficulties.

Consider "Resist not evil" (Matthew 5:39). Seemingly, according to this rule, we should not have resisted Hitler, a result I find unacceptable. If the rule is not meant to apply to a Hitler, we have been given no way of knowing it. So either way, it is not a good rule.

It may be argued that a distinction ought to be made between a result and a purpose: that the rule *does* apply to Hitler; that it undoubtedly aids the Hitlers of the world; but that this is not the purpose of the rule but merely a regrettable result that occurs from time to time; and that the rule is a good one, because it diminishes violence, even though it occasionally produces bad results. I do not find this convincing; I cannot give blind allegiance to a rule whose purpose is uncertain and that sometimes produces unmistakably bad results.

Let us look at another rule. Jesus said, ". . . Love your enemies . . ." (Matthew 5:44), but hardly anyone does. I do not see why I should love Mao, who has declared himself to be my enemy. If I assume that the purpose of this rule is to diminish hatred and cruelty, then I approve of the purpose; but I judge the rule to be ineffective, because almost no one obeys it; it is therefore not a good rule. Of course, I have merely *assumed* this aim; I do not know what the aim really is, because no aim is stated.

These are fatal defects in a moral system that is to be intellectually acceptable.

11. Requirements of a rule of morality; morality as means.

As the preceding section suggests, a rule of morality might be judged by (1) its purpose, and (2) its effectiveness. If it fulfills these two requirements—that is, if the results it aims at seem "good," and seem likely to be achieved—then we have a rational basis for finding the rule acceptable.

We will call this kind of morality "rational morality."

We have not yet said what we mean by "good." Nevertheless, we can say that rational morality will consist of rules or principles that seem likely to produce "good" results.

Thus morality—rational morality of the kind we hope to establish—is not an end in itself, but a means to an end: good results.

12. Morality as means (its historical justification).

There is historical justification for treating morality as means to an end.

When St. Thomas Aquinas defended the traditional rule against divorce, he did so by pointing out the bad results that would follow if the rules were abandoned. If marriage were not permanent, he said, fathers would have no part in the education of their children. This would be bad for the children, because fathers are more rational than mothers, and because they have the physical strength needed to administer punishment.

And when he defended the prohibition on incest, he did so on the ground that if the affection of brother and sister were added to that of husband and wife, the total would be so great that it would lead to an excess of passion.

We are not concerned here with the merits of these arguments, but with their nature: the rules are defended on the ground that they produce results considered "good" or avoid results considered "bad."

13. Morality as means (its advantage).

An important advantage of treating morality as a means rather than as an end is that it will be easier to get widespread agreement for such a system of morality.

For instance, everybody would probably agree that it is good to have adequate food and shelter and clothing, and that it would be good if everybody had enough of them. But not everyone would agree on the best way to accomplish this. The Russians would say that socialism does it best, the Americans would prefer private enterprise. So we would have the Russians and Americans agreeing on ends but not on means. As this indicates, it is easier to get men to agree on ends than on means.

Even when we disapprove of certain practices of former times, we find that our disapproval is based, not on the ends aimed at (of which we may still approve), but on the means used to achieve those ends; we do not think that the means formerly used are effective or even relevant.

> If we believed, as the ancient Spartans did, that homosexuality promotes courage in battle, we too might approve of homosexuality, since we want our soldiers to be brave.

> If we believed, as the Mayans did, that human sacrifice placates a god and thus avoids famine, then we too might approve of human sacrifice, since none of us wants to starve to death.

> If we still believed, as almost everyone did in the Middle Ages, that witches perform great evil, then we too might approve of putting them to death (as the Bible asks us to) before they have a chance to do further harm, since we wish to diminish the amount of evil in the world.

There is in fact a large measure of agreement among men as to what things in life are good. An ethic—and a morality—based on this can appeal to a large portion of mankind.

31

14. Ethics: various possible "goods."

We are seeking a morality that aims at results that are "good."

"What is 'good'?" is a very large question, probably the largest we can ask. The way we answer it indicates what we think the ultimate purpose of life should be; and it will determine many of the actions in our lives.

Many answers to the question have been offered over the centuries. They can be grouped in the following way:

It is good to obey the Will of God, or the voice of duty, or the promptings of conscience—and our actions should conform to such directives.

It is good to help or serve mankind (as Jesus and Buddha and the utilitarians advocated); our actions should be in harmony with this aim.

It is good to help or serve others—the "others" being some, but not all, of mankind, such as: our own family and friends, our fellow countrymen, members of our class, those who share our creed, those of the same culture, those with the same skin color, members of our own sex; our actions should serve the interests of the group we favor.

It is good that each of us should concentrate on himself, and aim to achieve virtue or glory or happiness or maximum pleasure or maximum development of potential capacities; our actions should serve this purpose.

These various "goods" can be stated in a less abstract way by imagining how a variety of people might explain why they had done a certain thing:

"I did it because it was God's Will," said the preacher.

"I did it because it was my duty," said the soldier.

"I did it for the sake of my conscience," said the draft card burner.

"I did it to help mankind," said the medical researcher.

"I did it for the sake of my children," said the father.

"I did it to benefit my friends," said the politician.

"I did it to strengthen belief in the power of prayer," said the priest.

"I did it to defend free enterprise," said the industrialist.

"I did it to help Labor," said the labor union official.

"I did it because I believe in complete equality for women," said the women's liberation propagandist.

"I did it to defend the white people of the country," said the southern senator.

"I did it to promote respect for policemen," said the police sergeant.

"I did it to help my fellow Americans," said the philanthropist.

"I did it because I hoped it would make me famous," said the sculptor.

"I did it because I wanted to become a better artist," said the painter.

"I did it because I thought it would make me happy," said the mountain climber.

"I did it for the pleasure of it," said the musician.

In all of these cases, people did certain things in order to achieve results they desired. The actions were means to ends —ends deemed to be good.

Insofar as people have different ends or aims or purposes, they also have different systems of morality. The man who cheats the government of taxes in order to accumulate more money to leave to his children has a system of morality different from the man who considers it his patriotic duty to pay every penny of taxes asked.

Since we seek a system of morality that will be workable, we must find one that can appeal to most (if not all) men. And for that, we must find some end or purpose or "good" that most men can agree on.

15. Merits of an ethic of happiness.

There are an impressive number of things to be said in favor of taking happiness as the goal of conduct—the happiness of all men impartially.

A morality that is hitched to an ethic of happiness would have the following desirable characteristics:

1. It is psychologically workable. It does not ask men to do what seems contrary to their nature, such as love their enemies or not desire a woman. On the contrary, it endorses and aims at the happiness that most men seek to achieve. To use the cliché, it "fits human nature."

2. It is understandable, in the sense of being non-mysterious. It does not serve some blind or hidden purpose which we are told is beyond our power to understand or asked to accept without understanding.

3. It is compatible with science. It does not require us to deny or ignore any of the findings of science, present or future. Nor does it require us to believe things for which there is no scientific evidence, that witches exist, for example.

4. It is universal. It is capable of appealing to all men equally because it is impartial. One man's happiness counts as much as another's; it favors no man or group; it excludes no man or group.

5. It serves everyone's self-interest, because it provides the best hope of achieving happiness for oneself, one's family and one's friends.

6. It accommodates both selfish and altruistic impulses.

7. It is conducive to survival in an H-bomb world.

The last three points need explanation. We will consider them in the next section.

35

16. Selfishness and altruism.

A man may give money to a charity because he feels sorry for people in trouble and wants to help them, or because giving money to charity will win him the community's praise and esteem, which he desires; the first motive is altruistic, the second selfish.

Similarly, I may send my son to college (as he wishes) for the sake of his future welfare or for the sake of my own prestige.

This shows that acts that are generally esteemed—and that, as we shall see, are morally right—can be motivated either by altruism or self-interest.

We can distinguish between two kinds of selfishness or self-interest:

1. Primitive or instinctive selfishness causes us to do things that benefit our families, our friends and ourselves —but not people we don't know.

2. Enlightened selfishness causes us to do things for the general welfare, things that benefit no particular person or group but everyone impartially. The motivation for doing this is something new in the world, and results from new conditions, namely, that it is no longer safe to ignore the desires or sufferings of others. Modern technology has made it possible for a relatively few discontented persons to inflict enormous damage on large numbers of people, in a way never before possible—in war, guerrilla warfare, riots, strikes; even a single dissatisfied or deranged individual, on a killing rampage, can do great harm before he is stopped. Today, everyone's safety and well-being is tied to the safety and well-being of all, in a way that was not true in the past. It is therefore part of enlightened selfishness to work for the general welfare.

Altruistic impulses—that motivate the things we do for others, out of feelings of love, affection, sympathy, compassion, or benevolence—have been affected by modern technology also; they have been given a greater reach. Television has made every part of the world visible to us all, so that it is not as easy as in former times to be indifferent to the sufferings of people in remote places. There would not have been nearly as much feeling in America, against the Viet Nam war, if the suffering and damage inflicted by the war had not been seen on television.

Altruism sometimes rewards its practitioners in ways they had not foreseen. Quaker shopkeepers were the first to abandon haggling over prices; they thought it was dishonest to ask more for merchandise than they were really willing to take. Thus they acted in an altruistic way and against what appeared to be their own self-interest (profit). The fixed prices proved to be such a convenience to the public that the Quaker shopkeepers prospered greatly. (Other shopkeepers eventually followed suit.) Thus, the Quaker shopkeepers' true self-interest was better served by altruism than it would have been by calculations based on apparent self-interest.

The Biblical injunction, "Love thy neighbor," presumably aims to overcome primitive selfishness and to promote altruism. If we take this to be its purpose, then it is plainly unsatisfactory as a rule of conduct (and of morality), since almost no one obeys it. But if "Love thy neighbor" is regarded, not as a rule of conduct, which is a means to an end, but as an end in itself—if "Love thy neighbor" is regarded as an emotional state or attitude (which is valued for itself) in which a man feels affection for, or goodwill towards, his neighbor and genuine concern for his neighbor's welfare—then it states a goal which is highly desirable, and likely to contribute to happiness.

*   *   *

In spite of these considerations, few people are able to achieve altruism in the present state of the world. And so, since most of us will act selfishly, we will, if we are wise, do so in an enlightened way; we will calculate as well as we possibly can where our true self-interest lies.

If, for instance, happiness is our goal, then whatever promotes our happiness is truly in our self-interest. But we do not always remember this. For example:

It is clearly in America's self-interest to have a treaty with Russia limiting nuclear armaments. The benefits are obvious and enormous: (1) a lessening of each side's fear of the other side's weapons, with a consequent lessening of tension and of the chance of nuclear war; and (2) a huge saving in armaments cost, freeing funds that can be usefully put to work on problems of pollution, ghettos, education, public transportation, etc. Both benefits would contribute greatly to our happiness.

But we don't like the way the Russians behave from time to time, as when they invaded Czechoslovakia in 1969. To show our disapproval and anger (and possibly also because our national pride was wounded, for we were powerless to stop the Russians), we decided not to meet with the Russians that year (1969) for purposes of limiting nuclear arms.

We presumably reasoned as follows: "To agree to limit armaments would help the Russians; it would make them more secure, for we would renounce our present freedom to develop improved weapons; and it would help them economically, for it would relieve them of the burden of spending money on new weapons. But we don't want to help the Russians—not now, at any rate, so soon after their bad behavior in Czechoslovakia. So we won't have a conference this year."

Our 1969 disapproval of the Russians' behavior blinded us to our true self-interest—which is, to promote our own happiness—and caused us to miscalculate. We preferred to deprive the Russians, even though it prevented us from getting what we wanted for ourselves; apparently we would rather hurt our enemies than help ourselves.

If we were to calculate our self-interest truly, we would sign a nuclear limitations treaty quickly, accept arms parity with Russia (instead of spending new billions to develop new weapons, to keep ahead of the Russians), and trade with Russia as much as possible— all of which would serve our own interests and contribute to our own happiness (as well as theirs).

If all this is so, it is evident that rational morality (based on an ethic of happiness) accommodates selfish motives (as well as altruistic ones), and seems likely to serve everyone's (primitive) self-interest, and is conducive to survival in an H-bomb world.

17. Impartiality; the morally right act.

If conduct is to aim to make men happy, all men impartially—if one man's happiness counts as much as another's—our aim would be to produce as much happiness as possible, without regard for who enjoyed it.

If we had to choose between two courses of action, the one that seemed likely to produce more happiness would be the morally right course to pursue. If a corporation wished to distribute Christmas bonuses, and could afford to give either (a) a large bonus to supervisory employees and nothing to production workers, or (b) a small bonus to all employees, it seems quite probable that course (b) would produce more happiness, and therefore, in this system of morality, would be the right course to take.

Thus an act would be morally "right" if it seemed likely to produce more "good" (more happiness) than any other available course of action. Any other act, in the circumstances, would be "wrong."

18. The morally right act.

To sum up the present position:

According to this system of morality, we would judge an action to be "moral"—"morally right"—if, of all possible acts in the circumstances, it seemed likely to produce the most happiness (or the least unhappiness), no matter whose. And we would judge any other action in the circumstances "immoral"—"morally wrong."

How do we know what acts will produce most happiness? How shall we recognize such acts when we see them? What do we know about the causes of happiness?

Before considering such questions, let us digress briefly, to consider an aspect of man's nature that causes him many difficulties and has a bearing on morality.

19. Social morality and private morality.

There are times when a man wishes to be with others, and times when he wishes to be alone. He is neither always gregarious, like ants and bees, nor always solitary, like lions and tigers. He is a semi-gregarious animal; some of his impulses and desires are social, some are solitary.

The social part of his nature is shown by the fact that solitary confinement is severe punishment. The solitary part appears in love of privacy and unwillingness to talk with strangers. People in crowded cities protect themselves against unwelcome intrusions by not speaking to the stranger sitting next to them on the bus; but if something alarming occurs, like an accident, they begin to feel friendly toward each other, and talk freely. This shows the oscillation between the private and social parts of human nature.

If we were completely social, the way ants are, we would always act to further the interests of the community; but we are not. That is why we need ethics, to keep us mindful of the community's interests, and moral laws to provide corresponding rules of action.

But if we could bring ourselves to be as submissive to the public interest as the ant—if we were willing to be completely "regimented" for the good of the community—we would not feel completely satisfied, but would feel that part of our nature that seems important was being starved.

Many great men whose innovations have changed the world for the better—mystics, poets, artists, scientific discoverers—have been essentially solitary. What such men do may be useful to others, and its usefulness may be an encouragement to them, but at those moments when they feel most alive, performing their chosen function, they are not thinking of the rest of mankind but are pursuing a private vision.

Each of the two parts of man's nature makes its claim. If morality is to "fit human nature," it must make allowances for both parts.

✓ ✓ ✓

The kind of conduct that the community as a whole considers desirable or acceptable reflects the community's standard of morality.

Most members of the community accept the community's standard of conduct; they conform. What they approve and disapprove, what their consciences approve and disapprove, is in harmony with what most other members of the community approve and disapprove—in keeping with the gregarious part of their nature. But some people, because of emotional or intellectual differences, have consciences or convictions that differ from the general average. If you have an exceptional dislike for the infliction of pain, you may become an antivivisectionist or may work to abolish prize fights; if you have a strong aversion to killing, you may become a vegetarian or a conscientious objector.

In such ways, a man's conscience may differ from his neighbor's. And on occasion he may find the praise and blame of his conscience more powerful and more compelling than the praise and blame of the community; the private or solitary part of his nature overrides the social or gregarious part; and he follows his conscience, in opposition to the community.

The kind of morality we are chiefly concerned with in this investigation is social morality. But the point must be made that there is more to morality than social morality. An ethic that recognizes only the social part, and does not acknowledge the private part, will be incomplete and unsatisfying. We need social morality to get along with the community, and private morality to get along with ourselves. Most of the time, fortunately, the two are in harmony; but occasionally, for some individuals, they are not.

A practical question remains: How shall a community treat an individual who defies it by following a private morality? Most of the worthwhile innovations, and contributions to civilization, have been the work of non-conformists. It would therefore seem to be in society's long-range self-interest to tolerate its eccentrics to the greatest extent possible, as long as its own security and continued existence are not endangered.

20. Requirements of happiness.

What makes for happiness is not properly a question for ethics or morals at all; it is a question for science. It can be investigated by scientific method, which, as everyone knows, is a method of exploring the unknown, by inventing hypotheses and testing them and discarding the ones that do not correctly predict the outcome.

Using this method, science would seek reliable hypotheses about the causes of happiness. Psychologists and psychiatrists and others have already learned a good deal about what is required for happiness. To be happy, most men require:

> the necessities of life (food, clothing, shelter); a minimum of security; friendship; love; a sense of belonging to some group; some satisfying work, in a job or outside it; good health; access to things that give pleasure, such as the arts, sports, the beauties of nature.

Also relevant are special causes of unhappiness, such as attaching undue importance to certain things; and various fears that have no basis in present reality.

It seems likely then that science can discover the means of producing *maximum* happiness. And morality would approve those means.

In sum, in this proposed system, *ethics* would tell us what the target is, namely, to produce the most happiness; *science* would tell us how to aim at the target; and *morality* would approve of what science tells us.

21. Morality based on happiness is not workable.

Have we now arrived at our desired goal of a rational morality that is (a) intellectually respectable, and (b) workable?

I find it intellectually respectable. It is understandable and non-mysterious, compatible with science, and contains no inner contradictions or inconsistencies.

But it runs into trouble on the point of being workable. Let us assume that science today can provide us with a reliable set of recommendations for producing happiness. Will people accept the recommendations?

The recommendations would constitute a new kind of pre-scribed morality, significantly different from the old kind, since it would have a known purpose instead of a mysterious one, a purpose that most men would find acceptable, and it would provide the most likely means of achieving its purpose.

Yet, despite these differences, there will always be many who won't want to be told what they want (or ought to want) in order to be happy. Their position is understandable. One childless couple may want very much to adopt a child; another couple may have no interest in children whatever. One man may want a steady job, that provides him with a steady income; another may want to work only when his money runs out, and to alternate periods of work with periods of leisure, not caring at all about a steady income. One man may care for music deeply, another not at all. The fact is, people have different temperaments, different needs, and different likes and dislikes. They all don't want the same things out of life—even though they may all wish equally to be happy.

Furthermore, scientific knowledge, never complete and never completely right, is always being revised. Science doesn't yet know all the answers to producing maximum happiness. A degree of mistrust of science, where it affects us in deeply personal matters, has theoretical justification, and should be respected.

So because of all this—because a man must be allowed to decide for himself what he needs for his own happiness—I conclude that this system of morality, that approves of the scientific prescription for happiness, is unworkable.

Even though men may agree on the goal of happiness, we will not be able to get them to agree on the means of achieving or pursuing that goal. We may get agreement on ends but not on means.

22. Differences and similarities of desires.

We have just discarded a morality based on a scientific prescription for happiness, for the reason that it cannot accommodate people who do not wish to follow the scientific prescription.

We said, in the previous section, that people don't all want the same things out of life, for no two people are completely identical.

But at the same time, neither are two people completely dissimilar. Both are members of the same biological species, and have certain characteristics—certain drives or motivations —in common, that produce similar desires.

In sum, there are both similarities and differences in the desires of different men. A system of morality, to be workable, must be able to accommodate the differences as well as the similarities. Let us therefore consider a system of morality that takes the satisfaction of desire (whatever the desire may be) as the goal of conduct.

23. Merits of an ethic that satisfies desire.

A system of morality based on the ethical goal of satisfying men's desires seems to have the following merits:

It avoids the pitfall of prescribing. Whatever a man may want is considered a "good" and each man's "good" is part of the "total good."

It accommodates those who choose happiness as their goal—those who desire to follow the scientific prescription for happiness and those who do not.

It accommodates those who do not desire happiness. A soldier may desire to do his duty. A seminarian may desire to obey the Will of God.

Additionally, it has all the merits claimed for a morality based on happiness, that is, it is psychologically workable, understandable and non-mysterious, compatible with science, impartial, serves everyone's self-interest, accommodates both selfish and altruistic impulses, and is conducive to survival in an H-bomb world.

According to this system of morality, an action would be judged moral or right if, of all actions possible in the circumstances, it seemed likely to produce the greatest quantity of satisfied desire (no matter whose). Any other act in the circumstances would be immoral.

I suggest that such a system of morality is both workable and intellectually respectable, and worthy of allegiance.

24. Satisfying desire, and happiness.

We have discarded as unworkable the ethical goal of producing maximum happiness; we have replaced it with the ethical goal of producing maximum satisfaction of desire. It is worth noting that men tend to be happy to the extent that their desires are satisfied. Therefore rational morality, in encouraging the production of maximum satisfaction of desire, is also encouraging the production of maximum happiness.

In rational morality, we regard satisfaction of desire as an end, a "good." But we can also regard satisfaction of desire as a means—to happiness.

Those who wish to may continue to regard mankind's happiness as the most worthwhile ultimate goal of action, and to regard satisfaction of desire as a means to that goal (as I do). In this way, the goal of maximum satisfaction of desire results in the kind of social morality most likely to produce the most happiness for mankind.

25. Satisfying desires; some questions.

Since we have chosen as our ethical goal the satisfaction of men's desires (to the maximum extent possible), we will then want to know: How can this goal be achieved?

This leads us to several further questions: What, in fact, are the things that men desire? What are the means of satisfying these desires?

Let us first consider what the things are that men desire.

26. Universal desires.

Men desire an infinite variety of things. They don't all desire the same things, but some desires seem common to all men. These include desires for the necessities of life: food, drink, clothing, shelter.

And, as already mentioned, most people also desire, for their happiness, some friendly companionship, a mate, a certain minimum of security, and a sense of belonging to some group.

It is because these desires are so nearly universal—and because most men would call the objects of these desires "good"—that we have a basis for a morality that can be universally accepted.

27. Three groups of desires.

We have just seen what it is that virtually all men desire.

In addition, some men also desire such things as fame, power, and great possessions.

Now let us consider what the means are—what the possibilities are—of satisfying men's desires.

We shall see that desires can be sorted into three groups.

The means of satisfying one of the groups is limited or unlimited, depending on circumstances that man can control.

The means of satisfying another of the groups is limited. The desires in this group cannot be satisfied, except partially. Furthermore, when some desires of this group are satisfied, they often interfere with the satisfaction of desires in the other groups. The desires in this group are the most troublesome.

The means of satisfying the remaining group is unlimited. All the desires in this group can, in theory, be wholly satisfied.

28. Compatible and incompatible desires.

Before going on to consider the means of satisfying desires, let us notice an important distinction in desires. Some pairs of desires are compatible, some are not.

If a man and a woman desire to marry each other, both desires can be satisfied. But if two men desire to marry the same woman, at least one of these desires cannot be satisfied.

If two partners desire the success of their firm, both desires can be satisfied. But if each of two rivals desires to be richer than the other, one of the two desires cannot be satisfied.

If two persons want to listen to the same radio concert, both desires can be satisfied. But if each of them wants to own the same oil painting, at least one of them must be disappointed.

What applies to two desires also applies to two groups of desires. When a nation is at war, the desires of its citizens for victory are mutually compatible; but these desires are incompatible with the opposite desires of the enemy.

Thus the desires of two or more individuals are compatible when they can all be satisfied by the same state of affairs. But when the satisfaction of one desire necessarily blocks or thwarts the satisfaction of another, the desires are incompatible.

Obviously, total satisfaction of desire will be greater when desires are compatible than when they are not. That is why, according to rational morality, love is preferable to hate, and peace to war.

29. Intensity of desire.

Desires are not all equal in strength or intensity.

If you desire to have apple pie for dinner tonight, and if you also desire to change your job, these two desires do not have the same intensity. If by some magic you were given the choice of having one of your two wishes granted, you would undoubtedly choose to change jobs rather than eat pie because you would consider the job more important to your continued well-being and happiness. In other words, your desire to change jobs is quantitatively greater than your desire for the pie, and if quantity of desire could be measured in some kind of units-of-desire, your job-desire would be represented by more units than your pie-desire.

In theory, rational morality takes into account the intensity or quantity of each individual's desires; but in practice it will rarely be possible to do this. Conceivably, at some future time, scientists may find a reliable correlation between some measurable characteristics of the human body and intensity of desire; perhaps the intensity of a particular glandular activity or nervous impulse will be found to correspond to intensity of desire; but this is a possibility for the future, not for today. Today we must usually assume that one individual's desire is quantitatively the same as another's, which is the equivalent of the "one man one vote" principle in politics.

Suppose four people want to go to the movies and there are two movies playing in town. They are all good friends, and wish to stay together, all going to the same movie. A, B, and C wish to see Movie #1, and the intensity of their desire can be described as a mild preference for Movie #1 over Movie #2. On the other hand, D has a very strong desire to see Movie #2, for unlike the others, he is a dedicated movie fan, and Movie #2 is directed by his favorite director and one of his favorite players has the lead. Using our imagined units-of-desire, if we say that A, B, and C each has a desire

54

of one unit to see Movie #1, and D has a desire of 5 units to see Movie #2, then 3 units of desire will be satisfied if all go to Movie #1, and 5 units will be satisfied if all go to Movie #2. Therefore more desire will be satisfied by going to Movie #2, and that, in theory, is the right thing to do. But if it is decided on the "one man one vote" principle, then the outcome will be the opposite—Movie #1 will prevail over Movie #2.

This shows that it is possible to produce the greatest good without benefiting the greatest number, or to benefit the greatest number without producing the greatest good. As already mentioned, rational morality, in theory, favors producing the greatest good, regardless of the number of people benefited. But in practice today, rational morality must accept the necessity of assuming that one person's "good" is quantitatively the same as another's, and therefore that the greatest good is produced when the greatest number is benefited.

30. The first group of desires—the desires for necessities.

To return to the means of satisfying desire:

The first group of desires we will consider are the desires for the necessities of life.

These are the most important desires because—since their satisfaction is necessary for survival—there is no limit to the efforts men will put forth, or to the violence they will use, in order to satisfy them. This group of desires provides the most powerful motives to action.

The desires for necessities are compatible or incompatible, depending on circumstances.

If two men, adrift in a lifeboat for days, have a tiny supply of water, each man's desire for the water is incompatible with the other's; whatever water is drunk by A is unavailable to B, and vice versa. But in ordinary circumstances ashore, where the water supply is adequate, each can satisfy his desire for water without in any way interfering with the other's ability to do the same.

As this shows, the desires for necessities are compatible when the supply is sufficient, and incompatible when it is insufficient.

The importance of this for our purpose is this: The necessities of life can be sufficiently supplied, at least in theory, to everyone today. Therefore, in theory, there need be no incompatible desires for the necessities of life. Of course, in practice, things are not like this, as reports of famine and wretched living conditions in many parts of the world indicate. An enormous increase of satisfaction of desire would result immediately, if everyone were supplied with enough of the necessities.

Our present theoretical ability to satisfy all desires for the necessities may not last indefinitely. If world population continues to grow at its present rate, it will one day not far off outgrow the food supply. That is why birth control is moral, according to rational morality; it will prevent a decrease in the satisfaction of the desires for necessities; prescribed morality, at least in its present Catholic version, calls it immoral.

31. The second group of desires—the incompatible desires.

We come now to the second group of desires, those that are flatly incompatible.

They cannot be fully satisfied because the supply (of what would satisfy them) is limited, and also because the desires themselves are unlimited; thus, for two reasons, they are insatiable. They are incompatible because their satisfaction, when it occurs, prevents the satisfaction of other desires, or of the same desire in others.

They are the desires produced by acquisitiveness, rivalry, vanity, and love of power.

✓　　　✓　　　✓

Acquisitiveness—the wish to possess as much as possible of money or gold, or stocks and bonds, or land, or works of art, or empire, or anything else—is obviously incompatible with the desires of others. It probably results from privations in childhood. If you didn't have enough to eat as a child, you may wish all the rest of your life to hoard. It is a motive of self-made millionaires who continue to work hard to make money long after they already have far more than they can spend. This is an important motive, especially among the powerful, because it is infinite; there is no limit on how much you may wish to amass.

✓　　　✓　　　✓

Rivalry, a still stronger motive, is the desire to outdo some other individual or group. It is what made America want to put a man on the moon before Russia did. It is what makes Ford want to beat General Motors in sales. It is by definition competitive, and therefore incompatible. Many of its forms are destructive, and that is when it is dangerous, as in blood feuds or war. It too is infinite; you will not be satisfied with having bested one rival, but will want to beat every-one else, until you alone are at the top of the heap.

✓   ✓   ✓

Vanity is a very powerful motive that shows itself in a desire for praise or attention or in a desire to avoid censure. Politicians, actors, and all who hire public relations firms may have a business or career motive for getting into the public spotlight, but they enjoy it for reasons of vanity. Vanity too is infinite; it grows with what it feeds on; the more you are talked about, the more you will wish to be talked about, which can lead you to do outrageous things. The desire for praise or attention is incompatible, for there is only a limited amount available; the man in today's newspaper head-line has made it unavailable to someone else.

Vanity is the chief cause of self-deception or unwillingness to face unpleasant facts, both in individuals and in whole nations or cultures. The Church forced Galileo to retract his belief that the earth moved around the sun instead of the sun around the earth, which was the prevailing view; it was un-acceptable to human vanity that the earth, with man on it, should not be at the center of the universe. America has tried to impose its ideas of democracy on parts of the world that have different conditions and traditions, and where they are unsuitable, as when we held an American type of "free elec-tion" in Viet Nam in 1966; it has been unacceptable to Ameri-can vanity that American political and economic institutions should not be exactly what the rest of mankind most dearly wishes to have.

✓   ✓   ✓

Love of power—the last and most important of the four motives we are discussing—is akin to vanity, but not the same. What vanity needs for its satisfaction is praise or glory, and they can be had without power. In England the King has more glory than the Prime Minister, but the Prime Minister has more power than the King. Like vanity, love of power is

59

insatiable, and nothing short of omnipotence can satisfy it completely. It is by far the strongest motive in the lives of important, energetic men, and the effect it has on the course of events is enormous and out of all proportion to its frequency.

In an autocratic regime, the holders of power become increasingly tyrannical, as they experience the delights of wielding power; and this also applies to petty power. Since power is experienced by making people do what they would rather not do, lovers of power are more likely to inflict pain than permit pleasure. If you ask your boss for permission to leave your office early, his love of power will get more satisfaction from saying no than from saying yes. That is why love of power is so dangerous.

✓   ✓   ✓

What, if anything, can be done about these four troublesome desires?

32. The incompatible desires can be managed.

The four desires in the second group—acquisitiveness, rivalry, vanity, and love of power—are not blind forces before which man is necessarily helpless. In theory, they can be eliminated, modified or managed.

✓   ✓   ✓

Acquisitiveness can probably be completely eliminated. When it occurs, it is usually found in people who spent their early years insecure in one way or another, which left them with a permanent anxiety about being deprived of what they consider essential in life. They may develop a fierce desire to save money or to hoard certain things. The way to eliminate acquisitiveness (in the next generation) is to eliminate the kinds of insecurity that cause it, which in theory is entirely feasible.

✓   ✓   ✓

Rivalry, vanity and love of power must be handled differently. They result from primitive, instinctive impulses and desires (often unconscious), and they neither can nor ought to be suppressed or eradicated, lest the life of impulse—which gives life its zest—be destroyed. The best ethical maxims are not ascetic or suppressive; they do not merely tell you what not to do; rather, they encourage and provide outlets that are constructive or at least not destructive.

✓   ✓   ✓

Rival countries, cultures and individuals can compete constructively to be first, for example, in finding cures for cancer and other ills. Or they can try to beat one another in Olympic Games, which produce much pleasurable excitement in a harmless way.

✓   ✓   ✓

Vanity—or at any rate, its excessive manifestations—results from humiliations or lack of adequate recognition, especially during early years. Napoleon, a poor scholarship student at the French equivalent of West Point, was snubbed by aristocratic fellow students, and in later life took immense satisfaction in achieving a glory that they could not; this is not a clear-cut case, however, since love of power was, with him, an even stronger motive. Vanity has a constructive side, and may be a motive of those who seek glory and fame through artistic and intellectual achievement.

✓   ✓   ✓

Love of power has done enormous harm in the world, but it has also done some good. It is probably the chief motive behind the pursuit of knowledge and advances in scientific technique. In politics it motivates the reformer as well as the dictator. Whether your love of power will lead you to do things that are good or bad depends on the social system (on the kinds of educational and career opportunities it provides) and on your capabilities. If your talents are theoretical or technical, you will probably contribute to knowledge or technique, and as a rule, your activity will be useful.

There has in fact been a great decrease in arbitrary power —of kings, slaveowners, husbands, and fathers—in Western nations during the past few centuries.

The harm that love of power can do can be minimized chiefly in two ways. One is to facilitate resistance by its victims; this is the method of democracy. The other is by education, so that love of power is led into channels that are generally useful, such as seeking power over nature through knowledge of natural laws, or power over men's minds through artistic or intellectual achievement. Even this course has its risks: knowledge of the laws of atomic physics has produced the H-bomb, which is not beneficial at all; and Nietzsche's doctrine of the superman acquired power over some men's minds and did great harm when it produced a belief in a superrace.

✓   ✓   ✓

To sum up: the four chief trouble-making desires are incompatible; and if allowed to flourish unchecked, necessarily lead to unsatisfied desires and, very often, to strife.

The ways in which a society can check or modify desires will be considered later. But no society—no matter what its makeup or institutions or code of morality—can ever wholly eliminate incompatible desires, even if that were thought desirable. There will always be two concertgoers competing for the same seat in the concert hall, two men wanting to outdo each other in something or other, or someone wanting to force his will on someone else.

But an enormous amount of presently competing desires can be eliminated, modified or managed—with a resulting enormous increase in satisfied desire and happiness.

33. The third group of desires—the compatible desires.

The third and last group of desires are the compatible desires—where one man's satisfaction does not interfere with another's.

These include a very wide range of "goods," including good health, the sheer pleasure of being alive on a fine day, friendship, love, travel, the enjoyment of natural wonders, pleasure in sports and games, delight in the creation or enjoyment of works of art and knowledge, etc.

In theory, these satisfactions can be universally enjoyed. And insofar as they are not, it is due to remediable defects in the social system, and presents no theoretical problem. Some of them require a certain minimum of leisure, education and income, a minimum which at present is not spread evenly throughout society. Rational morality, which aims to produce maximum satisfaction of desire—and hence encourages giving the widest possible scope to compatible desires, which are capable of virtually complete satisfaction—will approve of political measures aimed at giving the necessary leisure, education and income to all, which are the prerequisites for satisfying many of the compatible desires.

34. Theory of rational morality, summary.

We have now completed the theory of rational morality, which can be summed up in this way:

Rational morality aims to produce the maximum of satisfied desire. One man's satisfaction counts as much as another's, and it is therefore immaterial who enjoys the satisfaction; the aim is always to produce the maximum amount, no matter by whom enjoyed.

When we examine the nature of desires, to see how it might be possible to satisfy more of them, we find that (a) desires are either compatible or incompatible, and also that (b) desires can be sorted, according to our ability to satisfy them, into three groups.

An incompatible desire, if satisfied, inevitably thwarts the satisfaction of another desire. A compatible desire, when satisfied, does not interfere with the satisfaction of another desire.

The desires in the first group—the desires for necessities —are compatible or incompatible, depending on whether the supply is adequate to satisfy them all. They can, in theory, all be satisfied.

The desires in the second group—motivated by acquisitiveness, rivalry, vanity, and love of power—are unalterably incompatible, as well as insatiable. These desires, along with the desires for necessities, have been the chief causes of large-scale suffering—resulting from wars, foreign occupations, and slavery. They can, in theory, be modified, managed, or eliminated.

The desires in the third group—the desire to enjoy friendship, love, art, nature, creative activity, etc.—are compatible, and include most of what makes life seem worth living. In theory, these can all be virtually completely satisfied.

As a result, incompatible desires can be made to play a far smaller role in the lives of men than in the past, and compatible desires a far larger role—with a consequent very considerable increase in the total of satisfied desire.

Rational morality will therefore favor all measures that seem likely to increase compatible desires and their satisfactions, or to decrease incompatible desires or the scope of their destructiveness, for such measures will increase the total of satisfied desire.

Since rational morality will approve of some measures or actions and disapprove of others, it provides a standard by which to judge actions moral or immoral.

I suggest that we now have a sound, consistent basis for telling right from wrong.

We must now consider how it might be put into practice.

35. Putting theory into practice: harmonizing desires.

The attempt to promote compatible desires and to discourage incompatible ones can be stated in another way: it is the attempt to harmonize desires, so that what a man does in pursuit of the satisfaction of his own desires also satisfies (or at least does not thwart) the desires of others.

The tailor makes clothing in order to earn money, in pursuit of the satisfaction of his own desires; and the clothing he makes for others satisfies some of their desires. This shows that one way to bring the individual's desires into harmony with the community's is through the economic system.

Whether there is more harmony, or less harmony, in a society depends largely on the nature of that society, that is, on the way it functions.

Clearly people behave differently in an anarchic community, such as a mining town during a gold rush, from the way they behave in a community where the criminal law is well established and enforced. In an anarchic community, personal success is likely to be achieved through cunning, brutality and quick violence; in a well-ordered community, personal success will usually be the reward of actions that are thought useful. The methods used to become leader of a gang of outlaws are different from those used to become a college president.

↗   ↗   ↗

In considering the nature of a society, the three chief factors that make for more harmony—or for less—are (1) the nature of individual desires, (2) the nature of certain social institutions, and (3) the standards of praise and blame, embodied in the moral code.

↗   ↗   ↗

In considering the first factor—the nature of individual desires—we will distinguish between existing desires and future desires. Existing desires are influenced by the other two factors—social institutions and the moral code. Future desires can be greatly affected by the way the next generation is raised and educated, and questions like the following become relevant:

> What standard of morality or values is presented to the young? Is their attention directed to the benefits of cooperating with others? . . . or is it the man who gets ahead (of his fellows) who is admired? Is the potentially dangerous impulse of rivalry (competitiveness) led into useful or at least harmless channels, like trying to do a better job than someone else, or participating in competitive sports? Is the potentially even more dangerous impulse to power directed along socially useful paths that lead, for instance, to power over Nature through the acquisition of new scientific knowledge?

Few would deny that adult desires depend greatly on the ideals, attitudes, and habits acquired during the early years of life.

✓　　✓　　✓

Social institutions—the second of the three factors—refers to all the accepted ways in which a society gets things done: how it educates its citizens, produces and distributes its goods and services, raises its revenues, acquires its leaders, makes and enforces its laws, handles news and information, conducts its foreign affairs, etc.

Social institutions in America, for example, would include: compulsory education, public schools, private enterprise ("capitalism"), the graduated income tax, the secret ballot, a free press, 50 state legislatures and a Congress making laws, a foreign service headed by novices, etc. The relevance of this, for our purposes, is that many social institutions can directly affect the desires and actions of the individual members of the society.

If, for instance, a society's system of production enables

68

it to offer goods and services that most of its citizens find attractive (which, speaking broadly, is true in America)— or if its educational and economic systems offer opportunities for career advancement—it tends to act as an incentive and to make people *desire* to work better.

If its system of law enforcement is such that men think they can "get away with" breaking the law, many of them will break it; but they behave differently when they believe the laws are efficiently enforced. When men believed that income tax laws were not effectively enforced, many cheated; but when, as recently, they began to believe that enforcement had become efficient—through the use, by the government, of computers to keep track of all payments to individuals— cheating diminished and tax collections rose. Similarly there is probably less speeding on highways today, now that radar has made it a relatively simple matter to detect speeders.

✓   ✓   ✓

As for standards of praise and blame: people like to be liked or praised and do not like to be censured or hated. By giving or withholding praise or blame, the community can exert great pressure on the individual, to do the things it approves of and wants done. We give medals and awards to firemen, policemen and soldiers who display exceptional bravery, and to scientists who make significant contributions to knowledge or technique, to show the community's approval. On the other hand, the threat of community disapproval— including fear of what the neighbors might say—has made many a man paint his house or contribute to charities more often than he otherwise might have.

✓   ✓   ✓

In these various ways—through education and through systems of rewards and punishments (via social institutions and the moral code)—society tries to form and modify the individual's desires, to bring them into harmony with the prevailing desires of the community. All societies make more or less use of these means, but they could be used in our own society far more deliberately and far more effectively than at present, and with far better results. Rational morality approves of all measures that tend to harmonize desires.

36. How rational morality functions: majority rule.

If Congress enacts a law making it a crime to dishonor the American flag, and if this law reflects the dominant desire of the American people, then it is morally wrong (as well as unlawful) to dishonor the flag. More desire is satisfied if the flag is not dishonored than if it is.

This illustrates the general rule of rational morality: the morally right act is the one that, in the circumstances, satisfies the most desire.

We assume that we usually satisfy the most desire when we satisfy the majority; this occasionally will not be true when a minority's desire is intense and the majority's desire is mild, as mentioned on page 55.

There are three limitations on majority rule, which we will now consider.

37. Limitation #1 on majority rule: compatibility.

In 1968 Congress refused to pass laws requiring the registration and licensing of guns.

Did Congress do right in so refusing?

I will assume that Congress' decision truly reflected the prevailing desire in the country; I assume that a majority considers that it is perfectly proper to own a gun, and that it is nobody's business (including the government's) who does. Therefore Congress' decision satisfied maximum desire.

Yet the prevailing desire is probably based on a miscalculation; it will probably not produce the result most people want. A gun can be used for attack or for defense. I assume that only a small minority, like the Minute Men or some militant blacks, wish to use guns for attack; the great majority, motivated by fear, want guns for self-defense, for personal safety. The average man, however, fearful and with a gun in his hand, is likely to be too quick to shoot, and is likely to kill or injure people who, but for his gun, would not be hurt. It therefore seems probable that permitting unregulated guns to be in private hands will produce less safety for all rather than more. If this is so, then guns produce a result which is the opposite of what is intended and desired. The desire for guns is incompatible with the desire for personal safety.

I assume, further, that the desire for personal safety is stronger than the desire for guns, for the latter are merely (and mistakenly) considered a means to the former.

Since both desires cannot be satisfied, we must choose to satisfy one or the other. The right act is the one that in the circumstances satisfies the most desire, which in this situation means satisfying the stronger of the two desires, the desire for personal safety. It is therefore wrong to satisfy the other desire, the desire for guns.

Congress therefore did wrong in refusing to enact gun control laws, for these probably would have thwarted an incompatible desire (to own guns) in favor of satisfying the stronger desire (for personal safety).

This illustrates the first limitation on majority rule. When the majority wants something that is incompatible with something else it wants even more, then the weaker desire must give way to the stronger. We will call this the principle of compatibility. It seems obvious that a society that satisfies the stronger of two incompatible desires will satisfy more desire than one that does not.

38. Limitation #2 on majority rule: non-interference.

Suppose I am a Christian missionary, and I wish to convert a certain Moslem to Christianity, but he does not wish to be converted. Suppose, further, that he tells me that he would be willing to be converted to Christianity if I were willing to be converted to Islam. Would I be willing to become a Moslem in order to make him a Christian? Certainly not; I am a missionary because I am so convinced of the superiority of my faith that I want to convert others to it. I would under no circumstances be willing to give it up.

This shows that what a man wants for himself is more important than what he wants for others, or what others want for him. My desire to do what I want to do without interference from others is usually stronger than my desire to interfere with others.

Therefore when only two persons are involved, more desire is usually satisfied when what each person desires for himself prevails over what the other wants for him.

But when many people are involved, as when the majority desires Blue Laws—such as the current Pennsylvania law that bans liquor from restaurants on Sundays; or if, say, the whole community wants the village atheist to go to church on Sundays—the reverse is true: more desire would be satisfied if what the majority wanted prevailed over what the minority wanted. But it is here that the principle of non-interference applies.

According to the principle of non-interference, what a man wants for himself takes precedence over what others may want for him. Only in this way can each individual be assured that what he wants for himself (which is what he wants *most*) will not be interfered with by others unnecessarily. It seems evident that a society that practices non-interference will satisfy more desire than one that does not; hence a wise society will do so.

The only exception to non-interference occurs when my

desire may harm or endanger or interfere with others, as when I want to drive my car at 100 miles per hour through crowded streets or when I want to build a campfire in the forest during an excessively dry spell.

In politics the principle of non-interference is called "liberty" or "freedom." It permits each man to pursue happiness the way he wishes to, without interference, except when what he wishes to do interferes with what others wish to do. Politically this principle, when accepted, is a safeguard against tyrannical government and against the tyranny of the majority. A limited application of the principle of non-interference is found in the Bill of Rights of the U.S. Constitution, which guarantees freedom (non-interference) in specified areas—freedom of speech, freedom of religion, freedom of assembly, etc., regardless of what the government or the majority may wish at a particular moment.

This, then, is the second limitation on majority rule.

39. Limitation #3 on majority rule: equality.

The third limitation on majority rule may be called the principle of equality.

Suppose there is a segregated community where the whites are in a majority and where schools for white children are superior to schools for black children. The black minority wants the quality of black education improved up to the quality of white education. This would cost money, and would send the tax rate up. The white majority does not want higher taxes.

Here we have incompatible desires—the (black) desire for better education vs. the (white) desire to prevent higher taxes. Since the whites are in the majority, preventing higher taxes would satisfy maximum desire; but here the principle of equality intervenes.

According to the principle of equality, no one should deny to others what he wants for himself. In this case, whites should not deny to the blacks the same quality of education that the whites want for themselves. Therefore the (minority) desire of the blacks should prevail over the (majority) desire of the whites, until this equality has been achieved.

The justification of the principle of equality is that inequality tends to generate desires that remain unsatisfied as long as the inequality persists. Hence inequality works against the aims of rational morality; the former produces unsatisfied desires, the latter aims to produce satisfied desires. Furthermore, inequality not only produces unsatisfied desire (i.e., discontent) in those who are deprived; it may also lead to strife, which then will probably also produce discontent in the non-deprived.

There is of course nothing novel in the idea of equality. In 1776 the American Declaration of Independence called it "self-evident, that all men are created equal . . ." to justify political acts against established authority, in pursuit of equality. In rational morality, we apply it, where appropriate, to suspend the customary authority of majority desire, in pursuit of equality; this eliminates an important source of unsatisfied desire.

The society that practices equality seems likely to produce a larger total of satisfied desire than one that does not. Hence a wise society will do so.

40. Summary of argument.

Before applying rational morality to some specific situations, let us restate briefly the various steps by which we have arrived at our present position.

Traditional morality in the West has had two chief bases, the Bible and conscience. The Bible says a number of things that are no longer believed, and can therefore no longer be respected as an infallible source of truth. Consciences differ, so they do not provide any common basis for agreement on rules of conduct; and if we are not to be at each other's throats, we must be able to agree on the rules.

This suggests that a system of morality, to be acceptable, must be (at least) intellectually respectable and workable.

Traditional morality gives rules of conduct, but no reasons; the purpose of a rule is not told, which causes difficulties. This indicates that rules might be acceptable if we knew and approved their purposes, and if they seemed likely to achieve them.

Thus morality—which consists of rules or principles of conduct—becomes a means of achieving purposes or ends that are deemed to be "good."

Various "goods" are mentioned. One of them, happiness, seems to offer many advantages. The means of producing happiness is a matter for scientific investigation (as are the means of producing any desired result); but many people still will not wish to follow anybody else's prescription for happiness, scientific or otherwise; each man must therefore be allowed to decide for himself what he desires for his own happiness. Thus, though men may agree on desiring happiness, they probably would not agree on the means of achieving it. Happiness as a goal is unworkable.

We get around this difficulty by taking satisfaction of desire as the goal (instead of happiness), noting that the more desire you satisfy, the more happiness you tend to produce.

According to our system of morality, called "rational morality," the act most likely to produce maximum satisfaction of desire in a particular situation is the right one; any other act is wrong.

This leads to an examination of desires and the means of satisfying them. We find that pairs or groups of desires are compatible or incompatible; and that more desire can be satisfied when desires are compatible than when incompatible. We also find that desires can be modified by social institutions (such as the criminal law or the economic system) and by the moral code (which determines praise and blame), or formed by early education.

A wise society will use these means to modify desires, discouraging incompatible desires and encouraging compatible desires and their satisfaction, so as to produce maximum satisfaction of desire, and consequently of happiness.

41. An objection to rational morality.

An objection to a morality that aims to satisfy desire is that it is not noble or inspiring, since many desires are not.

A glutton's desire for food, or a silly woman's desire to be admired or envied for her clothes, are desires whose satisfaction is considered "good," according to rational morality.

How can the satisfaction of such desires—which most of us would agree are not worthy of admiration—be entitled to favorable consideration in the calculus of morality? How can desires like these have any relation whatever to moral rectitude?

The answer is: everyone must be allowed to pursue happiness in his own way. You may not approve of what another man desires; he may not approve of what you desire; but you must both acknowledge each other's right to do as each of you pleases. The aim of (social) morality is to enable you to get along with your fellow man. You will not do so, if you insist on prescribing for him.

42. Another objection to rational morality.

Another objection to a morality that aims to satisfy desire is that some desires are not merely unworthy or base, but are plainly harmful to others, as when A desires to inflict pain on B.

How can the satisfaction of a desire like this be considered a "good"?

When we view A's desire, not in the context of the total situation, but solely from A's point of view, then it is possible to say that the satisfaction of A's desire is a "good." But when we view the total situation, then we must also take into account B's desire (not to be hurt) as well as the desires of normal people in the community (to prevent the deliberate infliction of pain); these desires are thwarted if A's desire is satisfied.

Thus more desire in the community will be satisfied if A does not hurt B than if he does; and since the right act is the one that satisfies the most desire, the morally right course of action is for A not to inflict pain on B.

43. Similarities of rational morality and prescribed morality.

Rational morality and prescribed morality in the West differ very considerably, as we have seen, but there are similarities:

> Both are interested in the welfare of all mankind, not just some portion of it. No one is excluded from concern.
>
> Both value altruism and sympathy and benevolence; yet both rely primarily on self-interest—motivated by promises of rewards and punishments—to govern behavior.
>
> Both promise happiness as the reward for compliance, one in Heaven, the other on earth.
>
> Both threaten incineration for non-compliance, one in Hell, the other by H-bomb. Rational morality does not actually *favor* H-bomb disaster as a proper penalty for non-compliance but rather predicts it as virtually certain, if principles such as those advocated by rational morality are not followed.

Applications

44. Is the war in Viet Nam moral?

Let us now see how rational morality can be applied in various circumstances.

In the following sections we will apply rational morality to actions of the recent and not-so-recent past.

✔   ✔   ✔

Is the war in Viet Nam moral or immoral?

It can be argued that the war is immoral on the following assumptions: probably half the people of America want the war to continue and half want it to stop; the North Vietnamese people want the war to stop; the South Vietnamese people want the war to stop, except a relatively small number in government or benefiting by the war; all the other governments of the world that have been heard from, excepting Australia but not excepting the Papal State, want the war to stop. If all this is so, then most of the world wants the war to stop, and more desire would be satisfied by stopping the war than by continuing it. The war is therefore immoral.

However even if the majority of mankind wanted the war to continue, rational morality would still call it immoral on the following grounds:

> The principle of non-interference applies. What the Vietnamese want for themselves should prevail over what others (including the Americans) want for them.
>
> The principle of equality applies. The USA, by intervening, is denying to the Vietnamese something that America enjoys itself: freedom from foreign intervention.
>
> The principle of incompatibility applies. The American desire for victory in the war (insofar as this desire exists) is economically incompatible with the American desire to take care of American domestic problems (including schools, ghettos, cities, pollution, inflation, bal-

85

ance of payments). Assuming the domestic desires to be stronger than the war desires, more American desire would be satisfied by ending the war than by continuing it.

The principle of incompatibility also applies in another way. When war is waged by a nuclear power, it can escalate into nuclear warfare, and this can extinguish life on earth. Since the desire to live is the most fundamental of desires—and since the existence of life is a prerequisite to the satisfaction of all other desires—war which endangers all life endangers all satisfaction of desire, and is incompatible with the course most likely to satisfy the most desire.

The American intervention in Viet Nam is immoral for any or all of these five reasons, according to rational morality. And the North Vietnamese, in resisting American intervention, are fighting a just war.

45. Is refusing to fight in Viet Nam moral?

Is refusing to fight in the Viet Nam war, on the grounds of conscience or moral conviction, right or wrong?

We have just seen that, according to rational morality, the war in Viet Nam is immoral. Nevertheless, the prevailing desire in America is, probably, that draftees should be willing to fight. If this is so, then it is wrong to refuse to fight, from the standpoint of social morality.

However, if an individual finds that his conscience or his moral convictions will not let him participate in the Viet Nam war because he considers it an immoral enterprise, then, from the point of view of his private morality, he is right in refusing to fight. For this he will probably receive the majority's censure and punishment.

46. Was it morally wrong to drop the A-bomb on Japan?

Was it morally wrong to drop the A-bomb on Japan?

If we believe that America was fighting a just war, in opposing the German-Japanese axis, that initiated the war and was trying to impose its will on other countries—a just war because American victory would satisfy more desire than it would thwart—then America's victory in the war was morally right, and whatever helped to bring it about was morally right, including the A-bomb.

The point has been made, that it wasn't necessary to use the Bomb to achieve victory, because Japan was very close to surrender even before the Bomb was used (which fact was said to be known to the American High Command), and that the use of the Bomb showed a callous disregard for human life (Japanese), and was therefore morally wrong. Let us assume an extreme case: let us say that just before the bombing, American estimates indicated that 100,000 Japanese would be killed and that one American soldier's life would be saved (because the war would be shortened) through use of the Bomb; was the decision to use the Bomb, in these assumed circumstances, moral? I believe most Americans would have called it moral; but most of the world might have thought otherwise, and if so, the action would have been immoral.

47. Is euthanasia wrong?

Are euthanasia killings right or wrong?

If we consider the desires only of the people directly involved in a euthanasia situation—the suffering, hopelessly ill patient, who wishes to be put out of his misery, and the members of his family, who also wish the suffering to end—then more desire will be satisfied by permitting euthanasia than by prohibiting it.

But if we take into account the desires of the community, and if the prevailing desire is against euthanasia, then more desire would be satisfied by prohibiting it than by permitting it. But if so, the principle of non-interference applies: what the dying man and his family want should prevail over what others may want for them.

Therefore, regardless of what the community wants, euthanasia killings are moral, according to rational morality.

↗   ↗   ↗

The issue of euthanasia provides a direct comparison between prescribed morality and rational morality. The rational argument favoring euthanasia is that it satisfies the desires of incurably ill sufferers (and their families), whose suffering will continue as long as they live. Euthanasia thus contributes to the net total of happiness in the world by diminishing the amount of suffering, as well as by satisfying the desires of those directly affected.

The traditional argument against euthanasia is the Commandment, "Thou shalt not kill." As with all prescribed morality, you are told how to behave but are not told why you should. "Thou shalt not kill" is excellent rational morality in most circumstances, since most people do not wish to live in a community where one man is free to kill another. But this consideration does not apply to euthanasia, any more than it does to killing in self-defense or in a war, two well-accepted exceptions to "Thou shalt not kill." In time, euthanasia will also probably come to be another accepted exception.

89

48. Was it moral to buy liquor from a bootlegger?

Was it moral or immoral to buy liquor from a bootlegger during Prohibition?

The law prohibiting alcoholic beverages ("Prohibition") was immoral, according to rational morality, because it violated the principle of non-interference. Furthermore, if it did not represent majority desire, which it may not have, it was also immoral for that reason too.

Must one observe an immoral law, and not buy liquor from a bootlegger?

Let us recall that prohibition had many undesirable (and probably unforeseen) side-effects: it enriched criminals who went into bootlegging; it gave criminals a foothold in government; it provided opportunities for bribery and blackmail; it corrupted many public officials; it bred general disrespect for law by demonstrating how law could be broken openly and with impunity; it demoralized law enforcement agencies; it encouraged immoderate drinking habits; it deprived the government of large tax revenues; it deprived the law-abiding liquor industry of its livelihood; it produced some dangerous liquor that poisoned people.

The desire to drink liquor, which required patronizing a bootlegger, was incompatible with the desire for what might broadly be called "good government"—or at least, government freed from the harmful side-effects of Prohibition. Assuming that the desire for good government was the stronger desire, it was wrong to satisfy the other desire, which thwarted it. That is, it was wrong to buy liquor from a bootlegger.

Of course, most people did buy liquor from bootleggers, and the situation—from the standpoint of good government —became quite unhealthy and dangerous. It was finally corrected—and conflicting desires were finally harmonized—by repealing Prohibition, so that the desire to drink alcoholic beverages no longer thwarted the desire to have law respected.

49. Is it wrong to ignore someone's cry for help?

Is it moral to ignore someone's cry for help?

We will consider two types of situations, one in which you could help at no danger to yourself (though at some inconvenience), and one in which you would endanger yourself in order to provide help.

Suppose a man is swimming in the lake and cries, "Help!" and you are in a position to throw him a lifesaver or a rope. There is little doubt that the community would want you to help the drowning man, and will in fact be outraged if you fail to do so in these circumstances. Hence more desire would be satisfied by helping than by not helping, and therefore helping would be morally right.

Even if we ignore the community's wishes in the matter, we get the same result, for if we have a case of conflicting desires—the drowning man's desire to be saved, and your desire not to be inconvenienced—the two opposing desires do not balance each other. His intense desire to be saved far outweighs your relatively mild desire not to be inconvenienced; more desire will thus be satisfied by helping him than by not; it is therefore moral to help him.

Now to consider the other type of situation: a man is drowning in a stormy sea, and there is a possibility of your rescuing him if you jump in after him, at considerable risk to your own life; or a man is trapped in a burning building, and you see a way of climbing up to get him that offers a chance of saving his life, but at a sizable risk to your own. Is it morally wrong not to risk your life to save his?

Most people admire bravery, praise it highly and want to see brave deeds performed. Therefore brave deeds satisfy desire—they do not thwart desire, except perhaps the desires of an envious few—and are therefore morally right. But I do not think we can say that a man who does not risk his life in an attempt to save someone else's is morally in the wrong, unless there are special reasons why he should take the risk. Captains are expected to be the last to leave sinking ships, firemen are expected to be brave at fires, coastguardsmen are expected to take risks in rescues at sea, doctors are expected to risk the dangers of epidemics in treating patients, but the average man is not expected to run such risks. In any event, it would never be right to *ignore* someone's cry for help; if you cannot provide the help personally, except at risk to yourself, and if you do not wish to take that risk, your obligation is to do what you can to see that help is provided in some other way.

50. Is it wrong to cheat on your taxes?

Is it morally wrong to cheat on your taxes?

There are two reasons why non-cheaters will want the moral code to disapprove of cheating.

First, cheating tends to increase the tax rate, since tax money has to be raised, and the non-cheaters therefore have to be taxed at a higher rate to make up for the cheaters. Non-cheaters therefore will want cheating to stop, in order to keep the tax rate from going up.

Second, the non-cheater—who feels under obligation to pay his taxes—is likely to envy or resent the cheater's "getting away with" not paying. These feelings generate desires to see an end to cheating.

Since there are normally more non-cheaters than cheaters, more desire will be satisfied if the moral code disapproves of cheating than if it approves. Hence cheating is immoral.

*   *   *

Here, incidentally, is an example of how society can exert pressure to discourage an incompatible desire. Suppose I have a desire to cheat on my taxes. (The desire is incompatible because the tax-collector and the community desire that I not cheat). But then I begin to think of the disgrace and of the criminal penalties if I am discovered cheating, and this prevents me from cheating. Thus the moral code (reflected in potential public censure) plus the criminal law have modified my original desire to cheat.

93

51. Is it wrong to take drugs?

Is it wrong to take drugs?

We will make a distinction between addictive drugs and non-addictive drugs.

Suppose that a drug is found, perhaps marijuana, that is non-addictive and has no permanent disabling effects of any kind. Is it wrong to take such a drug?

Limiting our considerations to America: probably the prevailing desire in America—with its Protestant ethic of hard work and its Puritanical fear of pleasure—would be against the use of any drug whatever, however harmless. If so, the principle of non-interference—that what a man wants for himself comes ahead of what others may want for him— would apply. From the standpoint of rational morality, there is no objection at all to the use of a non-addictive drug.

The situation is different in the case of addictive drugs. The person who takes addictive drugs may commit crimes to raise money for his drug habit, or may become a public charge. His actions may thus harm others, and therefore the principle of non-interference does not apply. Since prevailing desire is undoubtedly against the use of addictive drugs, it is morally wrong to use them.

If a man were rich enough to pay for his drugs and to hire guardians to make certain that he did no harm to other people, then the principle of non-interference would apply— provided the society were not in a state of war or other emergency, so that it did not matter if society's resources were used in this way. In this case, it would not be immoral to use addictive drugs.

52. Is it wrong to cheat on exams?

Is it wrong to cheat on exams?

This question can be divided into two questions, and we will consider them separately.

↗   ↗   ↗

1) Is it wrong to cheat on exams in ordinary circumstances, that is, when most students do not cheat and the cheater is the exception?

The public does not wish to be cheated, and would not approve of a school that tolerated it, for if cheating were tolerated, it might sanction the idea that cheating is an acceptable way of getting along, not only in school, but also in society afterwards. The school faculty will wish to stop cheating, for cheating makes exams worthless. Among students, the non-cheaters will wish to prevent cheating, because cheaters may get better grades on exams than non-cheaters. Thus, the prevailing desire of the public, of the faculty, and of the students is to stop cheating; which makes cheating morally wrong.

↗   ↗   ↗

2) Is it wrong to cheat on exams when virtually every other student is cheating?

Although non-cheaters normally far outnumber cheaters, cheaters were apparently in the majority at the Air Force Academy a few years ago. The defense of the cadets caught cheating was that "Everybody did it." What is the morality of cheating in these circumstances?

A student has three options here: (a) to cheat, (b) not to cheat and to remain silent about the cheating, (c) not to cheat, and to report the cheating.

The school officials, the Air Force, and the general public would of course desire that there be no cheating, because

95

cheating makes exams worthless and presumably the exams served the useful function of indicating who the potentially better pilots and navigators are. Courses (a) and (b) satisfy the desires of the cheaters only. Course (c) satisfies the desires of the school officials, the Air Force, the general public, and the non-cheaters, all of whom far outnumber the cheating students and whose desire is quantitatively far greater. Thus, even when everybody else in school is cheating, cheating is wrong.

✓ ✓ ✓

There are other reasons why cheating is undesirable. When you cheat, you cheat yourself of peace of mind, for you never know when your deception may be discovered; you cheat yourself of a feeling of personal worth, for you know you have gotten something by fraud; you cheat yourself of the satisfaction that comes with mastering a subject. All of this is incompatible with personal happiness; but it is unrelated to the main concern of rational morality—which is to enable people to get along with each other—and so we will consider it no further.

53. Is it morally right to punish criminals?

Is it morally right to punish criminals?

Punishment—as meted out by the criminal law—can have several possible aims.

One aim is to deter potential offenders. The criminal law says that if you steal, you'll be sent to jail. This keeps many people from stealing.

Another aim of punishment is to reform an offender, so that he does not repeat his misdeed. If you have been fined $25 for smoking on a bus, you will think twice before you do it again.

The criminal law is obviously not completely successful in its aims of deterring and reforming, or there would be no crime. Yet it is equally obvious that many men refrain from breaking the law because they fear the penalty. The criminal law achieves partial, if not total, deterrence.

Punishment, or the threat of punishment—via the criminal law—is one way in which the community exerts pressure on the individual to make him behave as it wishes. The public wishes, say, to prevent stealing. A potential offender might wish to steal, but he knows that if he is caught stealing, he will be punished; in view of this risk, he may lose his desire to steal. In this way, the criminal law uses punishment to modify the incompatible desire to steal—incompatible because it conflicts with the community's desire to prevent stealing. Rational morality approves of measures that decrease incompatible desire.

It is therefore morally right to use punishment in a way that seems likely to discourage illegal (criminal) behavior.

*   *   *

The question—How much punishment is needed to achieve significant deterrence?—is one for scientific investigation, and presents no theoretical problem. If you wish to deter illegal parking, you might start with a small fine. As the

97

weeks go by, you keep increasing the amount of the fine. In this way you discover what correlation, if any, exists between increasing the fine and decreasing illegal parking. You may discover, for instance, that a $1 fine is wholly ineffective; that a $10 fine decreased illegal parking by 50%; and that a $100 fine is no more effective than a $10 fine. In this case, you will have found that maximum deterrence is achieved with a fine of either $10 or $100.

Which one should you use, $10 or $100?

There will be some who favor the $100 fine, who will argue more or less as follows: "The illegal parker knew he was doing something wrong. He didn't care whether he endangered or inconvenienced others. I have no sympathy with him—he broke the law deliberately and selfishly, and deserves to suffer for it. I'd have no objection to making the fine even stiffer."

This point of view results from a third possible aim of punishment—to inflict a penalty as the price of a misdeed. On this theory, wrongdoers must be made to suffer aside from any aim of reform or deterrence; punishment rewards them according to their deserts. This widely held belief, that punishment is payment of a debt to society—an eye for an eye— underlies much of our criminal law.

Since, on this theory, it is considered good that wrong-doers be made to suffer, it easily leads to the idea that the greater the suffering, the greater the good; this, in turn, leads to harsh penalties. That's why some people would prefer to impose a fine of $100 instead of $10.

We may now ask: Is it morally right to impose harsh penalties—punishment beyond what is needed to achieve reform or deterrence?

Some people feel it is right, others feel it is wrong; there is genuine moral disagreement, and no way of proving one side right and the other side wrong, except by finding out what the community desires. According to rational morality, if society wishes to impose harsh penalties, then it is morally right to do so; otherwise it is wrong.

✓   ✓   ✓

If society's prevailing desire is in favor of harsh penalties, I would argue against it in the following way, with a view to persuading the majority to change its mind:

The concept of punishment as payment for a misdeed is not useful. It is true that I must pay a fine when I am caught parking illegally, and it can therefore be said that I pay for my misdeed. But paying a penalty is not the same as paying for your dinner in a restaurant. When you pay for your dinner, there is an exchange of values; money is exchanged for dinner. Prescribed morality regards punishment in the same way; you pay for your misdeed (which harmed society) with punishment (which harms you); there is an exchange of values. The punishment is related to *past* behavior. But it is better to have punishment related to *future* behavior. The quantity of punishment should not be related to the degree of seriousness of the crime; rather, its sole aim should be to counteract future temptations to crime. Punishment should be considered a regrettable necessity, a means of modifying future behavior, and the less of it needed the better. Those who believe that mankind's happiness is the highest ultimate good will approve of holding punishment to a minimum, for punishment diminishes the total of happiness in the world.

The kind of penalties a society prefers tells something about that society. A society that is fearful and discontented is likely to prefer harsh penalties. Its members, being unhappy themselves, are pleased to think that someone else is even unhappier than they; and the unhappier they can make the criminal, the more fortunate (and more virtuous) they feel by comparison. A happy society is likely to prefer mild punishments.

54. Is it morally wrong to build high-powered cars?

Is it morally wrong for Detroit to build high-powered cars (that go very much faster than the legal speed limit)?

The argument against high-powered cars goes more or less like this: Detroit has found that it is easier to sell high-powered cars than low-powered ones, so it concentrates on high-powered ones. But these are more dangerous; they are more likely to be driven faster (especially by the young), more likely to be involved in accidents, and are likely to be more severely damaged in accidents because of the higher speed. Therefore, Detroit, in pursuit of profits, is deliberately ignoring safety, selling cars that are unnecessarily dangerous, which is morally wrong.

What are the merits of this argument?

First we must find an answer to the question: Are high-powered cars more dangerous? This is a question of fact, not of moral theory.

Perhaps a statistical analysis of accidents would reveal whether high-powered cars are involved in more accidents, in proportion to their numbers, than low-powered ones.

Assuming that high-powered cars are judged more dangerous than low-powered ones, does it follow that building them is immoral?

Not necessarily. Danger alone—out of context—is not the yardstick. We consider many dangers to be acceptable risks because they accompany benefits not otherwise obtainable. Trains and planes and electricity kill many people every year, yet we do not consider them immoral.

Society must decide how much danger it wishes to tolerate in return for what it gets in the way of usefulness or convenience or economy or pleasure.

In the present case, society has not yet decided what degree of extra danger it is willing to accept in return for the pleasure or convenience of extra power under the hood.

Once this has been settled—by legislative action, or perhaps by referendum—then it would become immoral (as well as illegal) to build cars more powerful than this.

55. Is pleasure morally good or bad?

Let us now apply rational morality to some questions that in one way or another are related to morality.

✻   ✻   ✻

Is pleasure morally good or bad? Or more correctly: Is it morally right or wrong to experience or approve of pleasure?

Most people desire to experience pleasure—it is a major source or ingredient of happiness—and therefore more desire will be satisfied if pleasure is experienced than if it is not. Consequently, to experience or approve of pleasure is morally right.

56. Does the end justify the means?

Does the end justify the means?

According to rational morality, the right action is the one that in the circumstances seems likely to satisfy the most desire. An action is therefore judged right or wrong according to its probable results. It is only by taking results into account that we can decide whether an action is acceptable; the end—the probable outcome—determines whether the means is right.

The statement, "The end justifies the means," is usually used to make unpleasant situations seem pleasant or palatable. The Russian Bolsheviks justified all kinds of inhumane treatment of people who opposed them—peasants who objected to having their lands taken away, opponents of socialism, and others—on the ground that the end (the workers' paradise on earth) justified the means (killing or enslaving those who objected to bringing the workers' paradise into existence). Used in this way, this is an immoral doctrine, according to rational morality. The Bolsheviks who seized power in 1918 were a very small minority; they imposed their ideas on a country that did not want them. Their actions did not produce maximum satisfaction of desire, and were therefore morally wrong.

We say that (a) "The end justifies the means," as used by the Bolsheviks, is morally wrong. Yet we also say, in rational morality, (b) the estimated ends will determine whether the means are morally right. Is there a contradiction here? According to rational morality, the end does justify the means, but in one case only: when the end aimed at is the maximum satisfaction of desire. The Bolsheviks may have believed that the probable outcome of their activities would be a workers' paradise. The defect in their position, from the standpoint of rational morality, even if we assume that their estimate of the outcome was correct, is that most people did not want their kind of workers' paradise or their way of achieving it. Had the Bolsheviks come to power and stayed in power and achieved their goals through persuasion instead of through force, then the majority would have *wanted* all this to happen, and the actions would have produced maximum satisfaction of desire, and would have been morally right.

57. Is selfishness wrong?

Is selfishness wrong?

Whether selfish actions are right or not depends on whether they seem likely to produce maximum satisfaction of desire.

Earlier, we made a distinction between primitive selfishness and enlightened selfishness. In the former, we do things for our family or friends, and for ourselves (possibly also for our compatriots), ignoring the rest of the world. In the latter, we do things for the general welfare, on the theory that, under conditions of modern technology, the well-being of some of us is tied to the well-being of all of us.

Primitive selfishness, unlike enlightened selfishness, does not aim at satisfying the desires of all men impartially, and is not likely to produce maximum satisfaction of desire; therefore rational morality does not approve of it. Rational morality approves of enlightened selfishness.

The answer to the question therefore is: Selfishness is wrong when it is primitive selfishness, but right when it is enlightened selfishness.

58. Is human life sacred?

Is human life sacred? Is it morally right to regard human life as sacred?

The concept of sacredness comes from prescribed morality, where you are told what to do or what not to do, and you are expected to do as you're told. When David was moving the sacred Ark on a cart over a rough road, Uzzah thought the Ark might fall, so he held it to steady it. For this he was struck dead, in spite of his excellent motive. (II Samuel 6-9).

Something sacred is inviolable; the rules about it are to be observed at all costs, regardless of circumstances.

If human life were sacred, it would never be right to take human life, even in self-defense. Few people would be willing to accept these consequences.

In rational morality, nothing is sacred, for circumstances are never ignored. The right act is the one that *in the circumstances* seems likely to produce the maximum of satisfied desire.

The rational way to regard human life is to say, not that it is sacred, but that it is *valuable*. It is valuable because people attach value to it. It is morally wrong to take human life because, in most circumstances, more desire is satisfied if life is preserved than if it is not.

59. Do men have inalienable rights?

Do men have inalienable rights? Is it a true proposition in morals that men have inalienable rights?

The Declaration of Independence calls it a self-evident truth "that all men . . . are endowed by their Creator with certain inalienable rights, that among these are Life, Liberty and the pursuit of Happiness."

This 18th Century statement is based on John Locke's theory of the previous century, that certain rights reside in the people, and no government can properly take them away, because they are "natural rights" resulting from "natural law," derived from the way society was formed. The Declaration goes even further, and says the rights come from God, from which it would seem to follow that only God can take them away.

But there are no natural laws; there are only man-made laws. To say that rights are "natural" or God-given is equivalent in political theory to saying, in morals, that some things are sacred. This is not very convincing to modern ears; nor is there any way of settling disagreements as to what is "natural" or "God-given." I conclude that there are no such things as inalienable rights.

There is, however, a sound theoretical reason for a society's guaranteeing its citizens the rights of life, liberty, and the pursuit of happiness. The reason, simply, is that a society that does so is likely to satisfy more desire than one that does not.

60. Is man naturally good or naturally bad?

Is man naturally good or naturally bad?

The answer here depends on what is meant by "naturally."

The statement, "Man is naturally bad," means that man, if he follows the promptings of his impulses and desires, will inevitably do bad things—things that harm others or do not produce maximum satisfaction of desire.

The statement, "Man is naturally good," represents Rousseau's romantic belief that primitive man in a primitive environment acted in ways that were good, and that civilization had corrupted him.

Men have certainly done bad things as well as good things. In rational morality, bad actions are neither the inevitable result of man's "nature" nor the necessary result of civilization; man can, through the use of his intelligence—through the correct calculation of the consequences of actions—learn to do things that are good (i.e., that satisfy desire) instead of bad (i.e., that thwart desire).

Man is neither naturally good nor naturally bad. He does some good things and some bad things, and can learn to do more good ones and fewer bad ones.

61. Can human nature change?

Can human nature change?

It is difficult to say exactly what is meant by "human nature." If it refers to something inside of man that controls his behavior—much as a gyroscopic "automatic pilot" controls the direction of a ship's travel—then the statement, "Human nature cannot change," implies that human behavior cannot change, and this is clearly untrue. We know we can change human behavior by means of various rewards and penalties—including praise and blame, financial and other incentives, and legal punishment—and by education. Rational morality is, of course, based on the proposition that human behavior *can* be changed.

"Human nature" can also refer to our expectations about the way people behave. If someone says, "It is against human nature for a mother to kill her own child," what he means is that he doesn't expect mothers to act this way. But expectations are continually being revised, as psychologists and others who explore human conduct learn more about us. So in this sense, too, human nature changes.

62. The Ten Commandments

Let us apply rational morality to the most famous of all Western codes of morality—the Ten Commandments.

Do the Ten Commandments provide good rules of conduct, according to rational morality?

The first four Commandments can be considered together. They tell us not to put any gods ahead of God, not to worship idols, not to use God's name if we swear, and not to work on the Sabbath.

The question we wish to consider is this: If you conduct yourself in the manner prescribed by these Commandments, are you likely to produce maximum satisfaction of desire? The answer depends on the nature of the community.

If the people of the community accept and believe in these Commandments and therefore wish to act in accordance with them, then observing the Commandments *will* produce maximum satisfaction of desire, and the Commandments are "right" or "moral," according to rational morality.

If the people of the community do not believe in these Commandments, then their observance will *not* produce maximum satisfaction of desire, and the Commandments are "wrong" or "immoral," according to rational morality.

If some members of the community believe in the Commandments and some do not, then the situation is more complex. We must distinguish between (a) what each individual desires for himself, and (b) what he desires for others.

I may care to observe the Commandments myself, but I may not care whether other people observe them or not. If the majority of the community feels this way, then allowing each person to decide for himself (whether or not to observe the Commandments) will produce maximum satisfaction of desire, and is morally right.

Or I may desire to observe the Commandments myself, and I may also desire that everyone else observe them too. If the majority of the community feels this way, then the prevailing desire is that everyone observe the Commandments. Such desires produce Sunday Blue Laws; but as we have seen, Blue Laws are morally wrong, because of the principle of non-interference.

In both cases, then, allowing each person to decide for himself (whether or not to observe the first four Commandments) will produce maximum satisfaction of desire, and is morally right.

The Fifth Commandment says, "Honor thy father and thy mother. . . ." Here, too, we must make the distinction between what I want for myself and what I want for others. I may wish to honor my parents, and not care whether other people honor theirs or not. Or I may wish to honor my parents and also wish that other people honor theirs. Whichever of the two courses will satisfy the most desire—whichever, that is, the majority wishes—is the right thing to do, according to rational morality. It seems highly likely that the currently prevailing desire is to honor parents; if so, it would be moral to do so; and the force of public opinion—in this case, public censure—would be brought to bear on those who do not wish to honor their parents.

Three other Commandments can be considered together: the Sixth ("Thou shalt not kill"), the Eighth ("Thou shalt not steal"), and the Ninth ("Thou shalt not bear false witness"). Most people do not wish to be killed, stolen from, or lied about; these three Commandments are entirely in accord with prevailing desire, and therefore with rational morality.

The Seventh Commandment, "Thou shalt not commit adultery," operates in a most delicate area of human activity. For many people, the most important aspect of morality is as a regulator of sexual conduct; in fact, the term, "immorality," in public discussion, usually refers to some disapproved kind of sexual behavior, and only rarely to lying, bribery, cheating, stealing, killing, treating people harshly, etc. If we consider the question—Will more desire be satisfied by the observance or by the non-observance of this Commandment? —it seems very likely that the prevailing desire will be against adultery; and if so, then adultery is immoral. Conceivably, at some future time, if the institution of marriage is further modified—new attitudes toward divorce, birth control, and abortion have already modified it considerably—so that sexual activities outside of marriage come to be considered acceptable, the Seventh Commandment will seem like one more ancient taboo that is no longer thought relevant.

The Tenth Commandment says, "Thou shalt not covet thy neighbor's house . . . wife . . . ox . . . nor anything that is thy neighbor's. . . ." Unlike the other nine Commandments, this one aims at governing desire rather than conduct. It tells you not to desire what belongs to your neighbor. This seems to be rational advice, that accords with rational morality, for if you desire what belongs to your neighbor, your desire is incompatible with your neighbor's desire to keep what he has. So "Do not covet," if acted on, would reduce the amount of incompatible desire. Unfortunately, this Commandment does not tell how to get rid of covetous desires; desires do not usually respond to mere commands. It is therefore probably not effective in reducing the amount of covetous desire in the world, and in this way falls short of being an acceptable rule of conduct. By contrast, rational morality, to the extent that it succeeds in producing men who are satisfied and happy, is likely to be effective in reducing covetous desire, for the happy man is not envious and does not want what belongs to his neighbor.

✓   ✓   ✓

In this discussion of the Ten Commandments, we have been using a limited kind of rational morality, applicable only to that portion of the world whose cultures—and whose people's desires—have been influenced by the Old Testament. The area is large, and includes Europe, North and South America, and parts of Africa and Asia; yet, it does not include parts of the world that have enormous populations, such as China, India, and parts of Africa. Since we are interested in a rational morality that will have universal appeal and universal applicability, we must now reexamine the Ten Commandments from the standpoint of all mankind, remembering that a great segment of mankind has never accepted or lived by the Ten Commandments.

It is unlikely that men who have never accepted the Old Testament would wish to obey those Commandments that relate to the primacy of the Old Testament God. We must therefore eliminate the first four Commandments. The Fifth ("Honor thy father and thy mother") is probably universally desired, as are the Sixth, Seventh, Eighth and Ninth (prohibiting killing, adultery, stealing, lying). The Tenth (prohibiting coveting) can be interpreted as telling the poor not to envy the rich; since most of mankind is poor, most men would probably not wish to follow this instruction, so more desire would be satisfied by dropping this Commandment than by keeping it.

If all this is correct, then five of the Ten Commandments have universal validity, and five do not.

Of the five that do not, four refer to the particular God of the Old Testament and are in that sense not universal, and one deals not with conduct but with desire, which cannot be effectively commanded.

The five Commandments in harmony with rational morality are desirable, not because they come down to us from the hallowed past or because they come out of the Bible, but because their acceptance is likely to produce more satisfied desire and more happiness than their rejection.

Credo

Credo

The main ideas of rational morality can be set forth in the form of a credo, more or less as follows:

1. I believe that the highest good consists in satisfying mankind's desires, and that we ought to try to satisfy as much desire in the world as possible.
2. I believe that each man must be allowed to decide for himself what he wants out of life, and that his desires added to the desires of all the other individuals in the world make up the sum total of mankind's desires.
3. I believe that people tend to be happy to the extent that their desires are satisfied rather than thwarted, and that therefore when we increase the amount of satisfied desire in the world, we also tend to increase the amount of happiness in the world.
4. I believe that one man's desire or happiness counts as much as another's, and that when we try to increase the amount of satisfied desire or happiness in the world, it doesn't matter whose it is. The important thing is to increase the total amount.
5. I believe that the satisfaction of any desire is good; but the morally right act is the one that, of all possible acts in the circumstances, seems likely to produce the greatest quantity of satisfied desire; any other act in the circumstances is morally wrong.
6. I believe that all action is prompted by desire, and that some groups of desire are compatible and some are not. Compatible desires can all be satisfied by the same state of affairs. Desires are incompatible when the satisfaction of one necessarily thwarts the satisfaction of others. More desire can be satisfied when desires are compatible than when incompatible.
7. I believe that desires can be modified—through education, through social institutions, and through public opinion reflecting the moral code—so as to decrease

117

the amount of incompatible desire and to increase the amount of compatible desire, and the result will necessarily be a larger total of satisfied desire and of happiness.

8. I believe in working to bring about modifications of desire so that, in future, incompatible desires play a smaller role in human affairs, and compatible desires a larger role—so as to produce an increase in satisfied desire and human happiness, to the maximum extent possible.